Who You Callin' Chicken?

Photographs by **Stephen Green-Armytage**
Written by **Thea Feldman**

HARRY N. ABRAMS, INC., PUBLISHERS

Check out all these weird-looking birds!
What do you think they are?

1

2

3

Want to take a guess?

4

5

WYANDOTTE
Silver Laced Rooster

It's the Pullet Surprise!

They are ALL chickens! And so are
ALL of these birds!

POLISH
Golden Laced Rooster

POLISH
Silver Laced Rooster

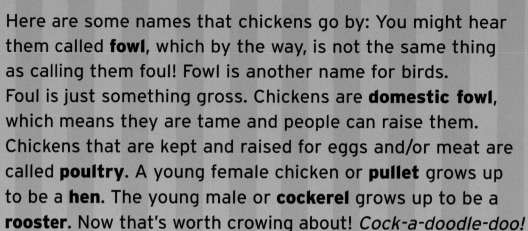

Here are some names that chickens go by: You might hear them called **fowl**, which by the way, is not the same thing as calling them foul! Fowl is another name for birds. Foul is just something gross. Chickens are **domestic fowl**, which means they are tame and people can raise them. Chickens that are kept and raised for eggs and/or meat are called **poultry**. A young female chicken or **pullet** grows up to be a **hen**. The young male or **cockerel** grows up to be a **rooster**. Now that's worth crowing about! *Cock-a-doodle-doo!*

POLISH FRIZZLE
Bantam Bearded Blue Hen

BRABANT
Cuckoo Rooster

Take A Walk on the Wild Side.

The Red Jungle Fowl is the ancestor of all chickens.

Experts have traced the roots of today's domestic chicken back over 4,000 years to the wild Red Jungle Fowl found in Southeast Asia.

People began to tame chickens thousands of years ago. Chickens are now found all over the world because travelers took them for meat and eggs wherever they went–even on board sailing ships!

RED JUNGLE FOWL
Rooster

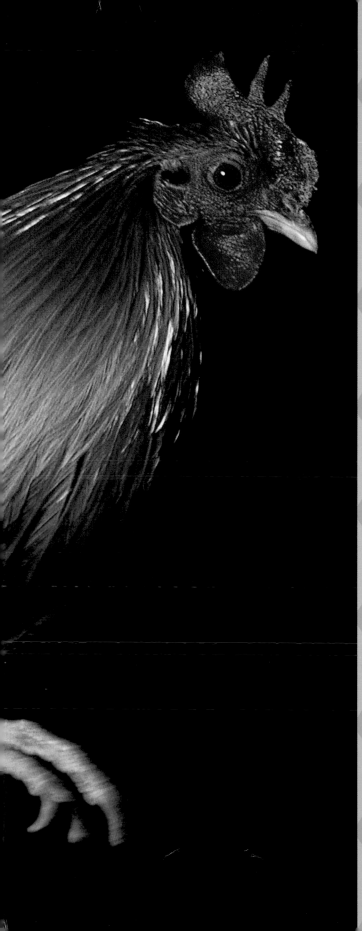

Don't Count Your Chickens!

There are hundreds of different kinds of chickens in the world today, including this Old English Game Chicken, which looks a lot like the Red Jungle Fowl.

OLD ENGLISH GAME
Black Breasted Red Rooster

It all adds up! There are over 200 different kinds or **breeds** of chickens in the world today. But the total number of individual chickens tops the 10 billion mark! Just think, that's more chickens than people on Planet Earth. Imagine if you had to give each and every one of them a name!

You're a Good Egg!

All chickens hatch from eggs. Chicken eggs can be a variety of different shapes and colors. It all depends on which kind of chick is waiting to hatch.

It takes about 21 days for a chick to hatch out of its eggshell, which can be white, different shades of brown, speckled, or even bluish-green.

A hen begins to lay eggs when she's only about 20 weeks of age. Hens exposed to 14-16 hours of light a day (either natural or artificial light) will lay more eggs.

Here a Chick, There a Chick . . .

What a traffic jam! All these cute little chicks will grow into a wide variety of breeds of chickens.

CUBALAYA
Black Breasted Red Chicks

Ready for action! Newborn chicks are able to see, eat, drink, and walk immediately after birth. They are covered in short, soft fluffy feathers called **down**. The down helps keep the chicks warm, which is very important for them to grow. So, getting down is a good thing for a chicken growing up!

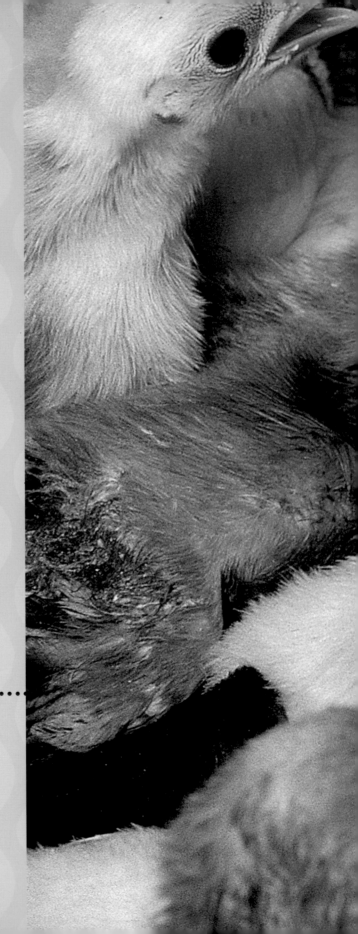

MIXED BANTAM CHICKS

What's Black or White and Bred All Over?

From plain to fancy, chicken breeds come in a spectrum of colors and patterns.

Some chickens are solid! Solid colors, that is. Depending on the breed, a chicken's **plumage** can be made up of all white, gray, black, or buff (tan) feathers.

ROSECOMB
Pearl Gray Rooster

SUMATRA
Black Rooster

LEGHORN
Bantam White Rooster

HAMBURG
Silver Spangled Rooster

SEBRIGHT
Silver Hen
(laced)

FRIESIAN
Lemon Penciled Hen

Some chickens have feathers with beautiful patterns on them that result in some pretty spectacular-looking birds. There's the penciled look (a variety of stripes on each feather), the spangled look (v-shapes on each feather), the mottled look (a different color on the tip of each feather), and so many more. It seems that chickens come in every pattern except for plaid!

COCHIN
Bantam Mottled Hen

A Tale of Feathers

There's more to a chicken feather than just its colors.
Its shape and length are important, too.

OLD ENGLISH GAME Red Pyle Pair,
Rooster (left) and Hen (right)

BELGIAN BEARDED D'UCCLE Gold Neck,
Hen (front) and Rooster (back)

YOKOHAMA
Red Shoulder Cockerel

PHOENIX
Golden Duckwing Rooster

You can often tell the difference between a male and a female chicken by looking at tail feathers. Females tend to have what look like well-trimmed tail feathers, while male tail feathers tend to be longer and look looser in styling. Some chickens, like the Japanese Yokohama, have very long tail feathers. And the Onagadoni (or Phoenix, which is also Japanese) has very, very, very long tail feathers, some of which grow to be as long as 18 feet! Now that's a really long tail tale!

Let's see how this shapes up! Chicken feathers come in different shapes and lengths. Feathers can be long and thin, short and fluffy at their base, or round and flat at the tip, to talk about just a few varieties.

Chicken Little!

Some chicken breeds are tall, and some are small, and sometimes there are big and little versions of the same breed.

LANGSHAN Black Rooster (left) and OLD ENGLISH GAME Bantam Black Rooster (right)

Hobbyists breed bantams to be about one quarter the weight of the standard for their breed.

BRAHMA Light Bantam Rooster (left) and Standard Rooster (right)

MINORCA
White Rooster (single)

WYANDOTTE
Partridge Hen (pea)

They may look like the good, the bad, and the ugly, but **combs** are standard-issue chicken headgear. And on their necks, chickens sport flashy **wattles**, purely for ornamental reasons. Hmm, maybe they *are* vain!

Meet the Combheads!

Every chicken comes with its own **comb**. Not because chickens are vain—these combs are part of their heads!

WYANDOTTE
White Cockerel (rose)

BRAHMA
Dark Rooster (cushion)

Comb shapes include the four basics: single, pea, rose, and cushion styles, but can also branch out into the more daring v-shaped or buttercup varieties.

SICILIAN BUTTERCUP
Rooster (buttercup)

Distinctive combs help distinguish one variety of chicken from another and are clearly quite decorative, as well. Usually bright red, combs can also be other colors, like black.

MINORCA
Black Hen
(single)

APPENZELLER SPITZHAUBEN
Silver Spangled Rooster (v-shaped)

Cock-a-doodle-COOL!

Some chickens sport huge puffs of feathers on their heads that look like punk rocker hairdos!

Talk about your head cases! These feathery hairdos called **crests** are the distinguishing feature of some breeds of chickens. Female crests tend to be rounder, while male crests tend to look more misshapen and wild.

APPENZELLER SPITZHAUBEN
Golden Spangled Rooster

POLISH
Golden Rooster

POLISH
Silver Laced Hen

FAVEROLLES
Salmon Hen (with beard)

Some crested birds go even further. They can have **muffs**, which are thick feathers puffing out on the sides of their faces. Or they can have **beards**, tufts of feathers on their throats. And somewhere underneath all those crests are neglected **combs**!

ARAUCANA
White Rooster (with muff)

OWLBEARD
Silver Spangled Rooster
(with beard)

Don't They Look Bent Out of Shape?!

These chickens may look like their feathers are bent the wrong way, but, in fact, they're not. They're curly!

PLYMOUTH ROCK FRIZZLE
Buff Rooster

Some chickens are naturally twisted. Chickens with curly feathers are called **frizzles**, but they are not a separate breed of bird. Frizzled chickens just have that distinctive look of feathers curling away from the body. It's just like people: some of us have curly hair, others don't. So, have you got frizzles straight?!

BRAHMA Hen (left) and Rooster (right)

You're A Star!

Some chickens compete in chicken shows held all around the world! They are judged for many different things including shape, color, and size.

LAKENVELDER
Rooster

PLYMOUTH ROCK
Barred Rooster

APPENZELLER SPITZHAUBEN
Golden Spangled Hen

To win at one of these shows you have to be a perfect chicken! Chickens and their owners have been feathering their nests with blue ribbons since 1845, when the first known major show took place in Regents Park Zoo in London, England.

The first United States show followed suit in 1849 in Boston.

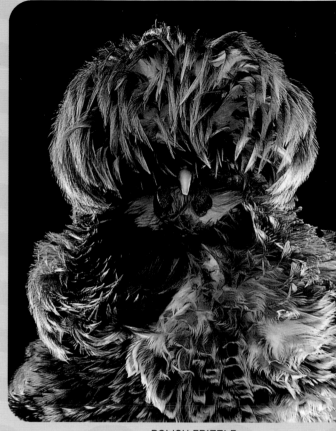

POLISH FRIZZLE
Chamois Rooster

Today, thousands of shows—big and small—are held each year. The American Poultry Association, founded in 1873, has published a book, *The American Standard of Perfection*, the definitive guide for judges and others, on all things chicken, since 1874.

So, while you may not be able to judge a book by its cover, you can definitely judge a chicken by the book!

POLISH FRIZZLE
Bantam White Rooster

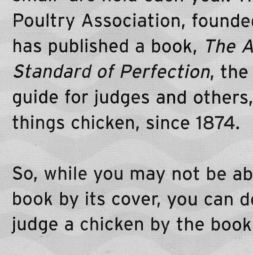

ORPINGTON
Buff Hen

SILKIE Gray Hen

OLD ENGLISH GAME
Bantam Black Rooster

Why Did the Chicken Cross the Road?

Have you ever really looked at a chicken's feet? They're pretty funny looking!

ARAUCANA
Rumpless Mottled Pullet

Maybe the chicken crossed the road to use its feet! Chickens have long toes that help them balance and to do all that running around that they do. Most chickens have four toes on each foot, but some have five. And some chickens have their toes hidden under feathers that cover their feet. Male chickens have a sharp **spur** behind each foot that they can use to defend themselves against other male chickens.

We Don't Have Lift-off!
Chickens are not good flyers. They get around best on foot.

MODERN GAME Black Breasted Red Cockerel

What? Chickens are birds, right? And birds fly, right? Well, that's mostly right. While most birds fly, some, like penguins and ostriches never get off the ground at all. Chickens can get their short, rounded wings working enough to carry them only a few hundred feet. So their preferred method of travel is by using their long legs. And, from the look of things, it seems like sometimes they just feel like dancing!

ARAUCANA
Mottled Pullet

WYANDOTTE
Bantam Silver Laced Hen

Fowl Ball!

Some chickens just look born to party—formal style! These chickens look ready to head off to a dress ball or night on the town. After all, they've just entertained you, so now it's their turn to have some fun. And if there's one thing you've learned about chickens, it's that where they're concerned, anything goes!

PLYMOUTH ROCK FRIZZLE
White Hen

ARAUCANA
Silver Duckwing Rooster

ARAUCANA
Silver Duckwing Rooster

Glossary

beard   a tuft of feathers on a bird's throat

breed   visibly similar in most characteristics, a group of birds related by descent from common ancestors

chicken   a species of domestic fowl

cockerel   a male domestic fowl less than a year old

comb   a fleshy crest on the head of a domestic fowl

crest   a showy tuft of feathers on the head of a bird

domestic fowl   any of various birds domesticated by humans to live and breed in a tame condition

down   a covering of soft, fluffy feathers

fowl   a bird of any kind

frizzle   a variety of chicken with curly feathers

hen   an adult female domestic fowl

muff   a cluster of feathers on the side of the face of some domestic fowls

plumage   the feathers of a bird

poultry   domesticated birds kept for eggs or meat

pullet   a female domestic fowl less than a year old

rooster   an adult male domestic fowl

spur   a stiff, sharp spine on the back of a male domestic fowl's leg

wattle   a fleshy, pendulous piece of skin that hangs beneath a domestic fowl's beak

....

To Whiskers, who always appreciated chickens in her own way.   – T.F.

Text copyright © 2003 Thea Feldman
Photographs copyright © 2003 Stephen Green-Armytage

Library of Congress Cataloging-in-Publication Data

Feldman, Thea.
  Who you callin' chicken? / written by Thea Feldman ; photographs by
Stephen Green-Armytage.
     p. cm.
Summary: Explores a wide variety of plain and fancy chicken breeds,
examining their feathers, life cycle, evolution, and more.
  ISBN 0-8109-4593-2
1. Chickens–Miscellanea–Juvenile literature. [1.Chickens–Miscellanea.]
I. Green-Armytage, Stephen, ill. II. Title.

SF487.5.F45 2003
636.5'0022'2–dc21

2003003831

Harry N. Abrams, Inc.
100 Fifth Avenue
New York, N.Y. 10011
www.abramsbooks.com

Abrams is a subsidiary of

LA MARTINIÈRE
G R O U P E

Printed and bound in China
10 9 8 7 6 5 4 3 2 1